REA… Y

The non… spects of busi… s writing

Joanna Gutmann

Readability

Published by Blue Ocean Publishing

www.blueoceanpublishing.biz

Typesetting by Norman Brownsword, Spitfire Design

A catalogue record for this book is available from the British Library.

ISBN 978-1-907527-40-1

Contents

Readability

A presenter who looks ill-prepared and disorganised, speaking in a monotone, will distract and bore the audience, leaving them confused and yawning. The presenter needs to look professional and use voice tone with pauses to hold the audience's attention.

A business writer needs to present ideas in a document which is inviting to read and easy to understand. Ease of understanding is partly the use of appropriate language and plain English, but it is also 'voice tone' – the correct use of punctuation. Punctuation and presentation work together bring your writing alive and help the reader understand your message.

Punctuation

Crack the punctuation code!

Clear guidance to help you understand the purpose of all the little dots and squiggles.

Tips and techniques to help you use each correctly to add voice tone to your words.

Presentation

Present documents to ensure they invite readers to read, sending a non-verbal message of ease and interest.

Keep your readers' attention by avoiding common barriers, so they are not offered opportunities to be distracted.

Punctuation

Introduction

When listening to the spoken word, you understand what is being said through a combination of words and voice tone. This tone will tell you the difference between the instruction and the question below:

> Can you get the report to me on Friday.
> Can you get the report to me on Friday?

In writing, that voice tone is communicated by punctuation. These little marks are a code and, if used correctly, will make your message clear to the reader. Used incorrectly, they will confuse the reader and reflect badly on you.

For many years, grammar and punctuation were removed from the academic curriculum which has resulted in many adults feeling 'stupid' because they don't know how to use the marks – sometimes don't even know what they are called. In 2013, punctuation tests were introduced at the end of Key Stage 2 and the teaching of the correct use of the marks returned.

Having been involved in business writing training for some twenty years, there is seldom a course that finishes without someone asking a question about punctuation. This has led to half- and one-day courses on the subject and now to this written guide.

For every mark, there are clear rules with examples to demonstrate their correct use. Work through them steadily, or use as a quick reference guide, as you prefer. Scribble in your own examples of correct (or incorrect) use if you want to make it relevant to your work.

Stop

Full stop .

A neutral close to an aspect of the subject, thought or idea.

Question mark ?

Where a direct question is asked of the reader.

Exclamation mark !

For emphasis or to indicate humour or surprise.

Full stop .

A full stop closes a sentence, unless it is a direct question or exclamation.

- A sentence must always make sense on its own.

Three full stops together (ellipsis) show where text is missing.

- Item 4.1 to be amended to read "...London and Bristol."
- Thank you for your letter of…

Full stops are not used with abbreviations.

- Mr J Khan
- Dr Jones is our GP
- Enc

Question mark ?

Use a question mark after a direct question.

- Where is Bowman Street?
- What time will she be back?

But not after an indirect question.

- He wanted to know how to find Bowman Street.
- She asked when you would be back.

Multiple questions need multiple question marks.

- Will you be attending the conference? Are you staying overnight? Would you like to attend the dinner?

Multiple questions are almost always better presented as bullet points.

Avoid phrasing an instruction as a question.

- Can you submit your leave summary before Friday.

If you mean to give an instruction, do so with both words and punctuation.

- Please submit your leave summary before Friday.

Exclamation mark !

Exclamation marks are best avoided for business documents. They are often seen as cynical or sarcastic and one person's joke is another person's irritation.

It is often unclear why the exclamation is 'something special'. For example, "The unit has treated 400 cases this month!" Is that good or bad? Higher or lower than expected?

Sentence hints

The dot at the bottom of the question or exclamation mark is the full stop, so you don't need another after it.

A sentence should be no more than 20 words (best calculated as an average over the document with an average of 18).

A sentence should be in one tense, generally in one timescale and, where different people are taking actions, they should take them in different sentences.

Got it? Test yourself

❶ Do you want the pack sent to all applicants

❷ The first applicant for the admin assistant post wanted to know if she would be entitled to a company car

❸ Jack wants to know if you want the pack sent to all applicants

❹ So that I can write up the report, can you tell me on what date was the initial complaint received, how many items did Mr Russell order, how many were faulty, what action did we take after that first letter

❺ Sarah hit the man

❻ Would you prefer red or blue

❼ Do you like the red or would you prefer blue

❽ Alison asked, "Can I claim expenses if I travel to the London office"

❾ Alice asked if she could claim expenses if she travelled to the London office

❿ Can I claim expenses if I travel to the London office

Pause

Comma ,

A short neutral pause.

Semi-colon ;

A longer pause, still neutral.

Colon :

A pause that introduces, often a list.

Dash -

A less formal introduction.

Comma ,

Don't use a comma if the sentence reads well without a pause.

A comma indicates a short pause.

- Although he caught the early train, he was too late.
- It is not the first conference he has addressed, but it is the most important.

The first possible place for a comma may not be best.

✗ The comma is a simple mark, but it is often over-used sprinkled through the sentence like confetti.

✓ The comma is a simple mark but it is often over-used, sprinkled through the sentence like confetti.

✗ Attack fire, if possible using an appliance provided.

✓ Attack fire if possible, using an appliance provided.

Commas can be used in pairs to 'bracket' text.

- The team discussed reducing the target, currently 98%, as it was felt to be unrealistic.

Make sure the sentence makes sense if you remove the text between the commas.

- The team discussed reducing the target as it was felt to be unrealistic.

Commas separate simple items in a list.

- Please bring the agenda, previous minutes and all papers.
- The service operates across Wiltshire, Somerset, Dorset and Devon.

There is no comma before 'and' or 'or' in a list, unless it is needed for clarity.

- We will provide three uniform shirts: pink, pale blue and navy and white.
- We will provide three uniform shirts: pink, pale blue and navy, and white.

It would be better to change the order of the items.

- We will provide three uniform shirts: navy and white, pink and pale blue.

There is comma before a quotation.

- She clearly said, "I appreciate that we will have to pay for this."
- The minutes show that the board, "...will support the application to be an approved centre."

If the sentence continues after the quotation, a comma is placed inside the quotation marks.

- "Investors in People has not made a significant difference," according to the Finance Director.

When you can use comma with 'and'

Where text is bracketed with commas and the 'and' falls next to the second comma.

- We will have four community centres, each in a dedicated building, and will offer services from some GP practices.

To add emphasis to a point.

- We have invested heavily in these laptops, and I want you to look after them.

If the word after the 'and' is not the linked subject that might be expected.

- The nurse will take a sample and check your blood pressure.
- The nurse will take a sample, and will let you know the result and your follow-up appointment.
- He had waited for an hour and a half.
- He had waited for an hour, and that was the cause of his complaint.

Semi-colon ;

It is a shame that the semi-colon and colon share the same 'surname' because it is the comma and the semi-colon that are related.

They are 'sisters'; the comma is quite small and insignificant, only getting noticed when in the wrong place. Semi-colon used to be the same but decided to make more of herself. After many hours in the gym, she has more presence (straighter shoulders, firmer muscles, more body mass); that's the dot on top of the comma – the same mark but with more presence.

Semi-colons are used in a sentence when a short pause (comma) is needed as well as a longer pause.

- Nick Simmonds is a senior engineer and qualified to undertake the work; he is on a year-long secondment to a hospital in Scotland, but will return for a week next month.
- Please obtain a medical report from your doctor, with a full explanation of the reason for your inability to work at present; this can be posted, faxed or emailed to us.

This short pause/longer pause may be needed in a list.

- The judging panel will be made up of Louiza Graczyk, Brigwood Academy; Jahida Kaur, Highbury College; Andy Selwood, Dundas 6th Form College; Amanda Fisher, Holmwood Secondary School.

Semi-colons can be used to group simple items in a long list. Group the items in some way that will be obvious to the reader and separate the groups with semi-colons.

- The report should include information from NatWest, Lloyds, Barclays; Debenhams, Next, Boots; Sainsbury's and Tesco.

A semi-colon is used to indicate a longer pause, often when the point of the sentence is to show contrast. It is generally best not to use a comma when it could be a full stop.

- Finance have the new laptops; HR will get them at the end of the month.
- Finance have the new laptops, they are finding them more reliable.

A semi-colon used in this way often replaces a full stop. If you cannot decide whether to use a semi-colon or comma, see if you can use a full stop. If you can, it should be a semi-colon.

✓ Finance have the new laptops. HR will get them next month.

✓ Finance have the new laptops; HR will get them next month.

✗ Finance have the new laptops, HR will get them next month.

In common usage, the last of these would be unlikely to cause offence.

Do not use a semi-colon with a conjunction. (but a comma is acceptable if you want to pause).

- The meeting lasted four hours; he was back for the presentation.
- The meeting lasted four hours, but he was back for the presentation.

Semi-colons can separate longer items in a list (gives the reader a bigger break between each).

- Sophie and Ed will take over the small and medium-size businesses; Toby and Ashran will be responsible for corporate clients; Benjamin will look after the public sector.

If there is a comma in any item in the list, use semi-colons to separate the items.

- Please bring an A4 pad; flipchart markers in a range of colours; two example documents, non- confidential in content; a laptop for note-taking.

Colon :

The colon introduces a list, replacing 'the following' or supporting it.

- Your policy does not cover the following:
    - fertility problems
    - pregnancy
    - childbirth
- Your policy does not cover:
    - fertility problems
    - pregnancy
    - childbirth

The colon can be used to introduce a list in a sentence if a pause is needed.

- Your policy does not cover the following: fertility problems, pregnancy or childbirth.

If no pause is needed, don't use the colon.

- Your policy does not cover fertility problems, pregnancy or childbirth.

The colon can also be used in a sentence if the first part strongly introduces the second.

- Eventually he admitted why he hadn't called the police: he'd left the back door open when he went to the pub.

Bullet points

There are three types of bullet points:

- where they are short enough to need no punctuation
- where they are longer, with pauses, they need punctuation;
- Where each is a separate sentence; the styles should not be mixed in one set of bullets! For this style, it is important that you cannot read from the introductory line into each bullet.

Where the introductory line leads into a simple list (under one line each, no pausing punctuation), nothing is needed after the introductory colon.

- Visitors are asked to:
    - respect the visiting times displayed at the ward entrance
    - bring only cold drinks onto the ward
    - avoid unnecessary noise and disturbance to patients

Where the introductory line leads into a list of more complex items (needing pausing punctuation), each should end in a semi-colon with a closing full stop.

- Visitors are asked to:
    - respect the visiting times displayed at the ward entrance;
    - bring only cold drinks onto the ward as hot drinks can represent a safety risk;

- avoid unnecessary noise and disturbance to patients, including the use of personal stereo equipment and mobile phones.

Where the introductory line is more like a heading, and does not 'read into' each item, treat each as a separate sentence (capital letter, full stop).

- Guidance for visitors:
    - Visiting is allowed during the hours displayed at the ward entrance.
    - Only bring cold drinks onto the ward as hot drinks can represent a safety risk.
    - Please avoid unnecessary noise and disturbance to patients, including the use of personal stereo equipment and mobile phones.

Dash –

The dash is similar to the colon in that it introduces, but it can only be used in a sentence (not to introduce bullet points). It is often used in email before a 'throwaway' remark and is generally only used in informal writing.

- It's a week to payday – no takeaway coffees for me!
- Thank you for your help – we met the deadline by 12 minutes.

Dashes can be used in pairs, working like brackets. See page 30 for more information.

Got it? Test yourself

Put the comma, semi-colon or colon if/where needed.

1. Please bring the manual ruler pens and pencils calculator and a dictionary.
2. Please bring the program disc a copy of the manual on which to make notes a 30cm ruler pens and pencils for taking notes and highlighting a scientific calculator and a dictionary.
3. In response to your comments I have arranged to meet all team leaders this week.
4. All team leaders have responded to the questionnaire with positive suggestions for preventing a recurrence of the fraud.
5. There are four teams remaining Barnsley Bath Halifax and Reading.
6. Staff are to get a small bonus this year directors have elected to receive nothing.
7. Have you ever received treatment for or related to back pain?
8. There are four teams remaining
    - Barnsley
    - Bath
    - Halifax
    - Reading
9. The Chief Executive thanked staff for "…the terrific efforts made to achieve the target."
10. The four remaining teams are Barnsley Bath Halifax and Reading.

Quotations

Quotation marks

“ ”

Indicate that the writer is using the exact words of another.

Ellipsis

...

Replace text in a quotation.

Square brackets

[ ]

Explain a word or phrase in a quotation.

Quotation marks

“ ”

Quotation marks are used to show that you are using someone else’s words. These might be attributed to a person or taken from a document.

- I have listened to the recording of the conversation and my colleague stated, “Cover is only provided if the hire car is authorised by the insurer.”
- Under the terms of your policy, “Cover is only provided if the hire car is authorised by the insurer.”

The capital letter and closing full stop are part of the quotation and are therefore within the quotation marks.

If the sentence continues after the quotation, a comma is used before the final mark.

- “It will be a white Christmas,” according to the weather forecast last night.

A quotation is usually a complete sentence, but if only part of the sentence is used, an ellipsis (...) indicates missing text. (See the next section for guidance on using the ellipsis.)

If you need to add an explanation within a quotation, use square brackets (see page 29).

Ellipsis ...

A quotation is usually a full sentence (or more); an ellipsis indicates that text has been omitted, it can be placed at the beginning or end (or both).

Place the ellipsis immediately after the opening quotation mark and joined to the first word...

- The chairperson said that the merger would be, "...sometime during the early part of the year."

...*or* joined to the last word, before the closing quotation mark.

- The chairperson said, "The merger would take place sometime during the early part of the year ..."

It's assumed that the initial capital letter or closing punctuation is included in the ellipsis, so the text starts with a lower-case letter or ends with no punctuation.

Quoting selectively from the sentence can change the emphasis.

- According to the finance report, "The pressure to reduce expenditure next year will affect all departments, irrespective of the savings already made."
- According to the finance report, pressure will be put on all departments, "...irrespective of the savings already made."
- According to the finance report, "The pressure to reduce expenditure next year will affect all departments ..."

See page 29 for the use of square brackets in a quotation.

Separate

Commas	, ,
Brackets	( )
Square brackets	[ ]
Dashes	– –
Inverted commas	‘ ’

Commas

, ,

A pair of commas is the 'lightest' separation of text, a pair of pauses often used to separate an aside.

Commas can be used in pairs to 'bracket' text.

- The team discussed reducing the target, currently 98%, as it was felt to be unrealistic.
- We will have four people at the exhibition, which is in Manchester this year, and three on long-term sick leave. There are not enough people to answer the phones.

Make sure the sentence makes sense if you remove the text between the commas.

- The team discussed reducing the target as it was felt to be unrealistic.
- We will have four people at the exhibition and three on long-term sick leave. There are not enough people to answer the phones.

Be careful not to accidently create this by using two commas in a sentence.

✗ Thank you for your booking, I have attached the confirmation, your receipt and travel information.

✓ Thank you for your booking; I have attached the confirmation, your receipt and travel information.

Brackets ( )

Brackets separate a group of words from the rest of the sentence (usually an explanation).

- The company has many self-employed customers who benefit from lower premiums (typically 15% less than employed individuals) because they make fewer claims.

The sentence must still make sense with the brackets removed.

- The company has many self-employed customers who benefit from lower premiums because they make fewer claims.

If the brackets fall at the end of the sentence, the full stop is outside them.

- The company has many self-employed customers who benefit from lower premiums because they make fewer claims (typically paying 15% less than employed individuals).

If the brackets form a separate sentence, the full stop is inside them.

- The company has many self-employed customers who benefit from lower premiums because they make fewer claims. (They typically pay 15% less than employed individuals.)

Square brackets [ ]

These are used within a quotation where you need to add some text to ensure the quote makes sense to your reader. This is usually a term like 'here', 'last year' or 'her'

Place the brackets immediately after the term you are explaining.

- Mr Walsh said, "I've had eight appointments here [hypertension clinic] and have never been seen on time."
- The minutes are clear, "The expenditure must be completed by the year end [2020]."
- According to the email, "The forms must be sent to him [Ben Carter] by 3.30pm on the closing date."
- Your policy states, "You are not covered for fertility problems [problems in conception or as a result of fertility treatment], pregnancy, childbirth or neonatal treatment."

Square brackets can be put in text to indicate where information would be placed.

- The heading for the chart is Missed Appointments [year].

This heading can be found towards the end of the readability section of this book on a line chart. In reality, the year would be given but I didn't want to put it in the example in order to future-proof the book.

Dashes – –

Dashes can be used in place of brackets, but only in the middle of a sentence.

- The company has many self-employed customers who benefit from lower premiums – typically 15% less than employed individuals – because they make fewer claims.

Because of the space around them, they are more intrusive and will place more emphasis on the information they contain.

- The company has many self-employed customers who benefit from lower premiums – typically 15% less than employed individuals – because they make fewer claims.
- The company has many self-employed customers who benefit from lower premiums (typically 15% less than employed individuals) because they make fewer claims.

Inverted commas

‘ ’

Use single inverted comas to indicate a title. If you prefer, you can use italics.

- You will find more information in ‘A Guide to Your Policy’.
- You will find more information in *A Guide to Your Policy.*
- In his report ‘Making Suppliers Supply’ John Smith suggests many ways of building relationships with our suppliers.

Inverted commas also indicate a specific use of a word or phrase.

- Although the dress code is ‘casual’, many people still wear a jacket.

Single inverted commas also indicate a foreign word that appears to be English.

- Our sales team usually book a ‘pension’ for the meeting in Spain.

Single inverted commas can indicate ‘humour’ (usually sarcasm!).

- Our ‘massive’ pay increase of 0.5%.

Punctuation is outside the inverted commas unless it is part of the title, etc

For rules for double inverted commas (see page 24).

Got it? Test yourself

1. I enclose a copy of My Employment, Terms and Conditions and would ask you to read through this before you start work with us.
2. The inspector's report draws attention to "large quantities of waste paper stored underneath desks."
3. Members of the new leadership team Chief Executive, Chief Operating Officer and Finance Director will attend and take questions from staff.
4. The tutor confirmed, "All students in the cohort (2019) understood what was wanted, and all were happy to comply with the course requirements".
5. The recording shows that Mr Azim said, I called customer services on the 23 March at 0942 and was told that a refund would be paid. In response, our team member checked the file and confirmed, I am able to refund the cost of the printer but not the delivery charge.
6. Mark Anderson denied the accusation saying I have only taken short tea and coffee breaks and a half-hour lunch break.
7. "There will be no strike action before Christmas, according to the union representative, unless there is further provocation from management."
8. All staff will be invited to attend although there will be no pressure to do so and will have the opportunity speak to the inspectors.
9. Mr Anderson said, "The training Practical Punctuation, will benefit all staff, it doesn't matter what they write."
10. You can reach us by bus the airport bus stops outside the door or by train with a short taxi ride.

Join

Hyphen -

Apostrophe ’

Hyphen -

It is difficult to give clear guidelines for the hyphen because its use is flexible and changes with time.

Out Patient ➤ out-patient ➤ outpatient

Wheeled chair ➤ wheel-chair ➤ wheelchair

If two (or more) words need to be 'glued' together to have the meaning you intend, a hyphen is the glue.

- Following an in-depth survey, the board have concluded...
- There was wall-to-wall coverage of the election.
- We should consider the discount for not-for-profit organisations.

Where a word is in two parts, joined by a commonly recognised letter pattern (eg ee, oo) it is better to use a hyphen.

- Co-operate (not cooperate)
- Mis-spelled (not misspelled)
- Re-enter (not reenter)

Fractions and numbers that comprise more than one word are usually hyphenated.

- Thirty-one
- Three-quarters

Where the prefix joins a main word that begins with a capital letter, use a hyphen.

- anti-British
- ex-Army

Different meanings of words that are otherwise spelt the same can be shown by a hyphen.

- Before he resigned, he re-signed our contracts.

A hyphen can be used to break words at the end of a line. Break at double letters or between syllables, taking pronunciation into account (never break a one-syllable word). Try to avoid using hyphens in this way as it can confuse the reader.

- Dis-satisfaction or dissatis-faction (not dissat-isfaction)
- Memor-able (not me-morable)

Apostrophe ’

Where letters are missing

The apostrophe shows where letters are missing where two (or three) words have been joined.

- That’s   that is
- Can’t   cannot
- O’clock   of the clock

Usually, it is only ‘its’ that causes a problem. If you can replace ‘its’ with ‘it is’ or ‘it has’ an apostrophe is needed.

- It’s not possible   it is not possible
- It’s been recommended that   it has been recommended that
- Its cover is missing   it is cover is missing – no!

Got it? Test yourself

❶ She is a white car fashionista. You can see her car from here with its go faster stripes and super size wheels.

❷ Mother to be attacked in front garden.

❸ We cant say it isnt ours – youve signed it on the final page.

❹ Theyre claiming that their right to live there is being ignored and we havnt been taking their complaint seriously.

❺ Staff will be offered one to one appointments with one of our in house trainers and an in depth handout will be provided for ongoing reference.

❻ Whos the idiot whose car got stuck under the barrier in the car park? Its not the first time a car has had its roof damaged that way.

❼ Mrs Patel has a walking stick but her post operative mobility is generally good.

❽ No one would cooperate with the enquiry and it was decided that it would be abandoned and the contracts would be resigned.

❾ Our signed for service: you can ask for your letter to be signed for at the time of posting to get evidence of delivery.

❿ Her ex husbands claim is strange as they had agreed to a no fault divorce and there was a pre nuptial agreement in place.

Apostrophe ’

To show possession

The origin of the apostrophe is unclear, but one suggestion (which makes sense with the rules below) is that it comes from an old English pattern of speech where both name and pronoun were used:

> *John his horse is in the field.*

Over time this became John’s horse, in the same way that did not can be joined to be didn’t, the apostrophe showing where letters are missing.

The apostrophe is a hook, seeing it warns the reader that the ‘s’ at the end of a word does not mean a plural, but that ownership is involved.

> We take our customers on an exciting tour.
>
> We take our customers’ privacy seriously.

There are a series of rules for the apostrophe:

> If the owner is singular, add the apostrophe and ‘s’.
>
> If the owner’s name ends in ‘s’ don’t add a second ‘s’.
>
> If the owner is plural and ends in ‘s’, just add an apostrophe.
>
> If the owner is plural and doesn’t end in ‘s’ add the apostrophe and ‘s’.

Got it? No? Not surprising as these rules don’t help much in reality. Read on for one simple apostrophe rule – the only one you’ll ever need.

The simple apostrophe rule

You need to be able to do two things: identify what is owned and identify the owner.

In the following examples the item owned is in italics.

Susans *desk*

Maxs *idea*

Now circle the owner.

- Susans desk
- Maxs idea

The apostrophe is placed on the circle

- Susan's desk
- Max's idea

This also works if the name ends in 's'.

- James desk
- Mrs Evans letter
- James' desk
- Mrs Evans' letter

It works for singular owners (above) and plural.

- Nurses training takes four years
- Callers irritation is evident.
- Nurses' training takes four years.
- Callers' irritation is evident.

Including plurals that don't end in 's'.

- The local childrens centre and womens refuge.
- Peoples respect for politicians has disappeared.
- The local children's centre and women's refuge.
- People's opinion of politicians has fallen.

It even works for acronyms.

- My GPs advice was to take paracetamol.
- GPs advice is usually to take paracetamol.
- My GP's advice was to take paracetamol.
- GPs' advice is usually to take paracetamol.

But make sure you don't put an apostrophe on a simple plural.

- GPs advise patients to take paracetamol.

You may also need an apostrophe to express time.

- Two weeks' leave

  But not on, "I'll be away for two weeks."

- A day's pay

  But not on, "We were paid for a day."

There is never an apostrophe on a pronoun
(a word that takes the place of a noun)

- Ben's office his office
- Is this file Kate's? is this file yours?
- The server's warning light its warning light

For guidance on using the apostrophe where letters are missed out, see page 36.

To test your use of apostrophes, see the 'test yourself' after the capital letter guidance below)

Capital letter

A

A capital letter starts a sentence. It is always needed after a question or exclamation mark, as well as a full stop.

Capital letters are used for proper nouns: the name of the person, place or thing, but not for common nouns (even if they share a word).

• The HR Department	the department
• Dr Nerys Carter	your doctor
• Whitchurch Hospital	the hospital
• XYZ NHS Trust	the trust
• The Finance Director	the director
• Oxford City Council	the council

Job titles are one of the most awkward areas when deciding when to use capitals or not. If you are directly replacing the person's name (or very closely linking it) with their job title, then capitalise it.

- Alex Kitchener reported...
- The Finance Director reported...
- Alex Kitchener, Finance Director.
- Alex Kitchener has been the finance director since the merger in 2018.
- Alex Kitchener has been a director since the merger in 2018.

Capital letters are usually used for acronyms such as GP or NHS. Take care to capitalise the letters correctly.

- GPs (more than one GP)
- GPS (global positioning system – satnav)

Days and months have capital letters, seasons do not.

- The committee will meet on the last Friday in March, April and May, but not again until the autumn.

Languages and people are capitalised.

- I like Italy, the Italians are friendly and Italian has been fun to learn.

Clinical conditions are only capitalised if named after someone.

- Hodgkin's lymphoma breast cancer
- Alzheimer's disease vascular dementia
- Asperger's syndrome autism

Trade names for drugs are capitalised, but not the generic names.

- Neurofen ibuprofen
- Prozac fluoxetine
- Valium diazepam

Start a quotation with a capital letter.

- According to this book, “Quotations should start with a capital letter unless an ellipsis is used to show missing text at the start of the sentence.”
- According to this book, quotations should start with a capital letter, “…unless an ellipsis is used to show missing text at the start of the sentence.”

Got it? Test yourself

1. According to Mrs Walls social worker, she and Mr Wall are going to separate.
2. The tube drivers strike is likely to cause disruption for three days.
3. The board discussed the issue of the trusts internet security and were concerned that each hospital had a separate virus protection program.
4. Over-performance across the CCGs has increased to 3.2%. The highest levels are seen in Elective Care, Critical Care and Day Case activity.
5. The NHSs approach to plastic surgery is not consistent and this is reflected in GPs advice.
6. The diagnosis of Parkinson's Disease led to his medication being changed to madopar although this was quickly changed to the generic version, co-beneldopa.
7. The Governments attitude to private healthcare has been influenced by the Telegraphs campaign after its readers letters showed their discontent.
8. Mrs Rafaels symptoms were apparent from last years assessment according to her gps notes.
9. Doctors training is no more rigorous than dentists but the public perceive it differently.
10. Your Doctor has recommended that you attend the above cardiac clinic. On your first visit you will be assessed by a specialist cardiac nurse and may also see your Specialist.

Presentation

Introduction

People are more likely to engage with you and listen to what you say if you look approachable; they are more likely to understand what you are saying if your non-verbal communication supports your words. 'Readability' is the term used for the same thing in writing: making a document looks approachable and ensuring your point is clear through the non-verbal presentation.

The rules for layout are not rule)s for rules' sake. Each one is there to achieve one or both of two purposes, that:

- when the reader first sees the document, it looks as though it will be easy to follow and understand, it actively invites the reader to start reading;
- as the reader moves through the document, every aspect of its presentation guides and supports their comprehension and does not place barriers in the way of it.

It was easy in the days when secretaries knew the rules and applied them automatically as they typed. Today, with everyone using computers, tablets and even audio voice-to-type, it is important to know how to use presentation to help your reader understand the point you are making.

Presentation is the term used to describe this invitation to the reader to read, and the support for their understanding as they do so. Although important for all readers, it also helps readers with dyslexia and visual impairment.

The presentation of a document also affects the reader's opinion of the writer on a subconscious (or even conscious) level. Sloppy presentation will indicate sloppy thought, a confused layout will indicate a confused brain and lack of care with presentation will suggest a lack of care with the accuracy of the content. A document which looks neat, consistent and easy to read may not draw attention to itself for these merits – it won't need to as the reader will already be involved in the content.

Using the book

Where there is comparison, you will find bad practice on the left page, corrected on the right page to show good practice. The text that is laid out in both versions usually explains the rule that is being applied.

The guidance is based on the general principles of 'readability' and on the guidelines of the excellent British Dyslexia Association. There will always be exceptions, people who simply have a personal preference for a particular layout, or someone with a form of dyslexia which means that an unusual presentation suits them. However, following the guidance will mean you please almost all of the people, almost all of the time and your documents will look as though you know what you are talking about.

Layout for dyslexia

The guidance for dyslexia is broadly the same as for general readability, with just a couple of exceptions.

Paper: The paper should be matt, cream or a soft pastel and sufficiently opaque to prevent seeing the text on the reverse.

> In the public sector, coloured paper may not be feasible, but economies have often meant the paper is off-white. If the paper is very thin, print on one side only.

Font: Use a plain font with even spacing, ideally Arial, Verdana, Tahoma, or Trebuchet. The font should be 12pt.

> Some readers may prefer 14pt, or even larger. This is one of the few areas where guidance conflicts with writing for non-dyslexic readers who may find this more difficult to read.

Colour: use dark text on a pale background. Be aware of colour-blindness, avoiding using red and green in particular.

Emphasis: Do not <u>underline</u>, use italics or type text in CAPITALS; save bold text for headings.

Headings: Scale headings to reflect their importance. Section headings should be larger than sub-section headings.

Layout: Left-align text with short paragraphs and wide margins; 1.5 line spacing is preferred. Bullet points are useful.

> The use of 1.5 line spacing is the second area where guidance may conflict as the extra space may not suit non-dyslexic readers.

Documents should be made available to readers with dyslexia in ordinary Word format (rather than PDF), so the layout can be changed to support their reading.

Typography

Typesetting

Football and rugby are both played with a ball, but the rules are very different as any junior footballer who picks up the ball and runs will find out.

It is the same for typesetting and typewriting: they are both letters on the page (or screen), but the rules are very different.

Typesetting is a term that has largely disappeared in the digital age, it refers to the 'setting of type'. Newspapers, magazines and books used to be 'set' by putting a block with the letter carved out between two holding bars to create each word. This was highly skilled work, as each piece had to be in place with every line ending in the same place; there was no time to edit/tidy, as the paper had to roll off the presses in time for the daily paper. Search YouTube for 'typesetting' for some videos of typesetters at work.

The rules for typesetting are different to those for business documents presented in the A4 format.

The font is much smaller, the information presented in narrow columns, the margins are justified, there is no blank space between paragraphs, the first paragraph is blocked and subsequent ones have a small indent.

Today, the lines between typesetting and typewriting have blurred, as type is used in different ways: email, web-design, business leaflets, etc.

The simplest guidance is that if a document is to be presented in the A4 format (eg a letter, report or minutes), the typewriting rules should be followed; where it is to be published (eg web page or newsletter) follow the typesetting principles.

Corporate house style should not try to combine the two because readability will suffer. Published documents do not look professional using the typewriting style and readers of business documents will find them harder to read if presented in the typesetting style. It is not difficult to create a common style with flexibility where needed to meet the needs of both.

Typewriting

Typewriting (now shortened to typing) is the term used to describe the presentation of business documents. It used to be achieved by pressing a key which sent a metal bar with a letter imprinted, to hit the page through an inked ribbon. Every letter and symbol took up the same space.

With the advent of computing, fonts have developed so each letter takes up the space it naturally needs – an 'n' takes less space than an 'm'. 'Kerning' moves the letters, so they are spaced consistently and according to their shape. On an old typewriter an 'm' and an 'i' took up the same space. Look at the three letters 'mid.' that follows: the 'i' is nearer to the 'm' than the 'd' and there is gap before the full stop: `mid.` Now look at it in the current font: mid.

However, business documents are read on A4 paper (or screens) and, if the typesetting rules are followed, are off-putting and difficult to follow.

The main differences between the rules for the two styles are that typesetting is justified, typewriting is not; typewriting has a blank line between paragraphs and they all start at the left margin; typesetting has one space after a sentence, typewriting has two; typewriting uses a larger font.

Don't worry if this is all too much to take in, the rules are explained separately on the following pages.

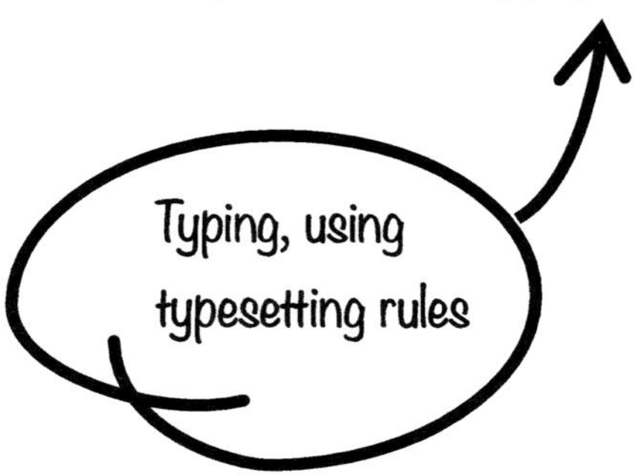

Typing

Typewriting (now shortened to typing) is the term used to describe the presentation of business documents. It used to be achieved by pressing a key which sent a metal bar with a letter imprinted to hit the page through an inked ribbon. Every letter and symbol took up the same space.

With the advent of computing, fonts have developed so each letter takes up the space it naturally needs – an 'n' takes less space than an 'm'. 'Kerning' moves the letters, so they are spaced consistently and according to their shape. On an old typewriter an 'm' and an 'i' took up the same space. Look at the three letters 'mid.' that follows: the 'i' is nearer to the 'm' than the 'd' and there is gap before the full stop: `mid.` Now look at it in the current font: mid.

However, business documents are read on A4 paper (or screens) and, if the typesetting rules are followed, are off-putting and difficult to follow.

The main differences between the rules for the two styles are that typesetting is justified, typewriting is not; typewriting has a blank line between paragraphs and they all start at the left margin; typesetting has one space after a sentence, typewriting has two; typewriting uses a larger font.

Don't worry if this is all too much to take in, the rules are explained separately on the following pages.

Don't justify text

Justified text looks neater because of the straight margins, but it can cause problems for some readers with dyslexia. These are usually described as the words moving, not staying still long enough to read, or just seeing a block or brick and not the individual words. Most readers find it harder to absorb the information when the text is justifiedand will be harder to read for almost everyone.

The first reason is that the size of space between the words, and even letters, will vary from one line to another, so the brain has to 'reset' itself at the start of each line. This unnatural spacing between words can make it difficult to see at a glance where a sentence ends. Larger spaces are more likely to line up vertically, making a white 'river' which divides the text unnaturally.

Have you ever been reading a magazine, read down to a picture and gone to start the next column? It can be several lines before you notice you've moved from one article to another; you should have continued the column under the picture to the bottom of the page. Your eyes are ahead of your brain when you are reading so by the time your brain realises something isn't quite right, your eyes are probably at the end of the paragraph. Most readers just carry on, not having the interest to go back and work out what was written. This is far more likely to happen if all the lines end in the same place.

Look at the size of the spaces on the first and second lines, compared with the third and fourth.

Left-align your text

Justified text looks neater because of the straight margins, but it can cause problems for some readers with dyslexia. These are usually described as the words moving, not staying still long enough to read, or just seeing a block or brick and not the individual words. Most readers find it harder to absorb the information when the text is justified.

The first reason is that the size of space between the words, and even letters, will vary from one line to another, so the brain has to 'reset' itself at the start of each line. This unnatural spacing between words can make it difficult to see at a glance where a sentence ends. Larger spaces are more likely to line up vertically, making a white 'river' which divides the text unnaturally.

Have you ever been reading a magazine, read down to a picture and gone to start the next column? It can be several lines before you notice you've moved from one article to another; you should have continued the column under the picture to the bottom of the page. Your eyes are ahead of your brain when you are reading so by the time your brain realises something isn't quite right, your eyes are probably at the end of the paragraph. Most readers just carry on, not having the interest to go back and work out what was written. This is far more likely to happen if all the lines end in the same place.

One space after a full stop is not enough

Your eyes are ahead of your brain when you are reading, as your brain needs to have the continuing words to process the meaning your eye might read 'the' 'report' 'will' 'be' 'late' – your eye has reached 'late' before your brain starts to work out the message, so it has all the words to play with and reads it as 'the report will be late' an important aspect of comprehension is being aware that the end of a sentence is approaching this helps the brain make sense of the words the eye is seeing the reader is able to keep up not have to catch up.

Did you have to read the paragraph above a couple of times to understand it? First to realise that there was no punctuation and second to work out what was meant. Did you realise too late that there should have been a full stop? There is often confusion over whether the 'two spaces after a full stop' rule is just old fashioned. It is suggested that it was relevant when each letter took the same space (see section on typesetting). In fact, it was perhaps less important then because the spaces were large and the full stop was small so 'dot space' gave quite a large gap.

With today's use of 'kerning' (moving letters so they take their necessary space), the 'dot' is very small and a space is narrower than the letter 'n', so two spaces is even more important.

The reality of most business documents is that they are full of capital letters (often overused and placed incorrectly), acronyms, symbols and numbers (capital-sized). With modern fonts such as Arial or Calibri it is difficult to see at a glance which mark is used so having two spaces after a full stop, when combined with the dot and the capital letter, gives a clear visual indication of a new sentence.

Two spaces to break up the paragraph

Your eyes are ahead of your brain when you are reading as your brain needs to have the continuing words to process the meaning. Your eye might read 'the' 'report' 'will' 'be' 'late' – your eye has reached 'late' before your brain starts to work out the message, so it has all the words to play with and reads it as 'the report will be late'. An important aspect of this comprehension is being aware that the end of a sentence is approaching. This helps the brain make sense of the words the eye is seeing; the reader is able to keep up, not have to catch up.

Now there is punctuation in the paragraph above, supported by appropriate spacing, it is easier to read at first glance. The 'two spaces after a full stop' rule is less important in books, newspapers and websites because there are fewer capital letters. Like on the last page (after the first paragraph) page, the 'dot, space, capital' is probably enough for most readers to see the end of a sentence approaching.

With today's use of 'kerning' (moving letters so they take their necessary space), the 'dot' is very small and a space is narrower than the letter 'n' so two spaces is even more important. This helps the eye to see where the sentence will end which helps the brain make sense of the information it is receiving. It is an important aspect of readability.

The reality of most business documents is that they are full of capital letters (often overused and placed incorrectly), acronyms, symbols and numbers (capital-sized). With modern fonts such as Arial or Calibri it is difficult to see at a glance which mark is used so having two spaces after a full stop, when combined with the dot and the capital letter, gives a clear visual indication of a new sentence.

Font

Don't use too small a font size

The 'font' is the style of type and it can be set to a variety of sizes. Don't be tempted to use a smaller font in order to get smaller paragraphs or fit more on a page; the text will just look too 'difficult'. It's like picking up a book at the airport, when you flick through the pages, type that is small or dense in appearance can just look too heavy for your light-hearted holiday mood. A long report is not going to look less off-putting for being typed in a small font to reduce the page count.

The actual size of the font can vary, so 12pt Times New Roman is noticeably smaller than 12pt Arial (see the examples on the next page to illustrate this). If you are using Times New Roman, it is best to make your minimum size 12pt. However, if you are using Arial, you can use 11 or 11.5pt and the text will still be legible.

Calibri is now the default font for Microsoft Word and is increasingly popular. Try to use a font where the letters are clear and easily recognisable. For example, 'g' not 'g'.

Avoid fonts such as Comic unless writing for children; many adults find them irritating and patronising.

The following are all 12pt. They look ridiculously large in a book, but are appropriate for documents in an A4 format. Note how much larger Arial is; you may want to use 11pt if this is your preferred font, but the others are better as 12pt.

Arial

The quick brown fox jumped over the lazy dog's back.

Calibri

The quick brown fox jumped over the lazy dog's back.

Times New Roman

The quick brown fox jumped over the lazy dog's back.

Arial 11pt

The quick brown fox jumped over the lazy dog's back.

A serif font?

A serif font is one where the letters have a small 'flick' at the beginning and end – known as the serif. Times New Roman is the most popular; it has been used for this paragraph.

Many people find these fonts old fashioned and prefer the crisper look of a sans-serif (without the serif) font. A sans-serif font is preferred for readers with dyslexia and those with visual impairment because it is crisper and less cluttered.

However, the little serifs create a subtle line which can help the reader's eye follow the line. A font like Times New Roman may be preferred by those who speedread.

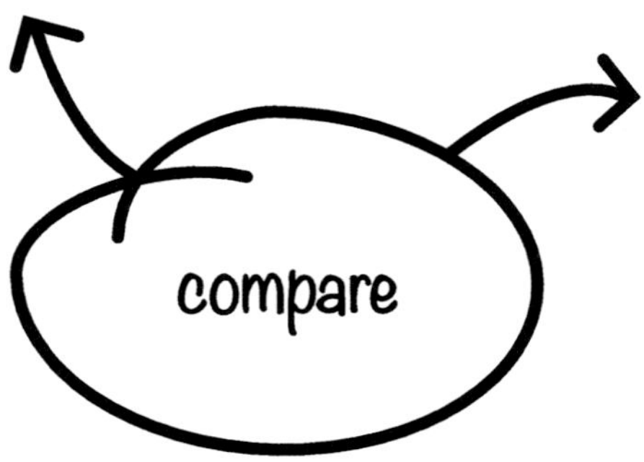

Or sans-serif?

A sans-serif font is one where the letters do not have the small 'flick' or serif. The most common is Arial or the more modern Calibri, but there are many styles in common use today. This paragraph has been typed in Arial.

Many people prefer the crisper look of a sans-serif font. It is preferred for readers with dyslexia and those with visual impairment because it is less cluttered with a cleaner shape.

However, the little serifs create a subtle line which can help the reader's eye follow the line. A font like Times New Roman may be preferred by those who speedread.

Wrongly-used capitals confuse the reader

Capitals are physically larger and both draw the eye and create a block to be passed. Many are incorrectly used, so the reader is getting contradictory messages of 'this is a name' (from the punctuation) and 'this is not a name' (from the text).

Example:

Barkinshaw NHS Trust has been working with Clinical Commissioning Groups (CCGs) in its geographic area to look at ways of improving the patient experience of those who use its Outpatient Services. The project was originally inspired by the Friends and Family Test (FFT), but was further developed by a team which included Consultants, Doctors and Nurses as well as Hospital Managers. An increased patient-focus has led the Trust to make many relatively small changes to the way its Hospitals operate, and its FFT rating has significantly improved.

Hint: Only give an acronym (eg CCG, FFT) where it will be used frequently in the following text. It can often be replaced by using the common noun (eg the test) on subsequent uses to reduce capital letters

Capitals for proper nouns, used to name

Example:

Barkinshaw NHS Trust has been working with clinical commissioning groups in its geographic area to look at ways of improving the patient experience of those who use its outpatient services. The project was originally inspired by the Friends and Family Test, but was further developed by a team which included consultants, doctors and nurses as well as hospital managers. An increased patient-focus has led the trust to make many relatively small changes to the way its hospitals operate, and its test rating has significantly improved.

Hint: Only use a capital when you name (Dr John Smith / Dr Smith / your doctor will advise), (Kent County Council / the council)

Clinical conditions only have a capital only when named after someone (Asperger's syndrome, Hodgkin's disease). Only brand names of drugs have a capital (Nurofen / ibuprofen)

Don't have long paragraphs

It is too simplistic to give a simple line count as guidance for a paragraph because the length should be based on the content. However, if the paragraph gets too long, the reader is likely to subconsciously switch off part way through and move on to the next one. A long paragraph looks off-putting and the reader may struggle to keep their eye on the line. Generally, five or six lines is a good maximum, but if there is just one more thing to say, one more sentence, an occasional eight-line paragraph should not cause a problem. If your paragraph is growing too long, keep writing until you finish all you have to say on the subject and then read back through it and look for places where the logic of the content determines the best place to break. If the content is familiar to the reader, the English plain and the punctuation good, the paragraph can be a little longer. If the reader is less familiar with the content, the paragraphs will need to be shorter.

Keep the paragraphs shorter

It is too simplistic to give a simple line count as guidance for a paragraph because the length should be based on the content. However, if the paragraph gets too long, the reader is likely to subconsciously switch off part way through and move on to the next one. A long paragraph looks off-putting and the reader may struggle to keep their eye on the line.

Generally, five or six lines is a good maximum, but if there is just one more thing to say, one more sentence, an occasional eight-line paragraph should not cause a problem. If your paragraph is growing too long, keep writing until you finish all you have to say on the subject and then read back through it and look for places where the logic of the content determines the best place to break.

If the content is familiar to the reader, the English plain and the punctuation good, the paragraph can be a little longer. If the reader is less familiar with the content, the paragraphs will need to be shorter.

Too many short paragraphs lose the 'flow'

Thank you for your letter regarding a claim as the result of the theft of your mobile phone.

The Bronze Policy excludes the theft of a phone from a car although we may consider a claim where the phone was locked out of sight.

I enclose a claim form; please complete this, giving a full explanation of the circumstances, and return it to me.

If the claim is accepted, no further claims of exceptional circumstances will be considered.

You may wish to consider increasing your level of cover for greater protection and I have also enclosed a leaflet detailing the policies we offer.

I look forward to receiving the completed claim form, but if you need any further explanation, or would like to increase the level of cover you have, please do not hesitate to contact me.

Link information that belongs together

Thank you for your letter regarding a claim as the result of the theft of your mobile phone.

The Bronze Policy excludes the theft of a phone from a car although we may consider a claim where the phone was locked out of sight. I enclose a claim form; please complete this, giving a full explanation of the circumstances, and return it to me.

If the claim is accepted, no further claims of exceptional circumstances will be considered. You may wish to consider increasing your level of cover for greater protection and I have also enclosed a leaflet detailing the policies we offer.

I look forward to receiving the completed claim form, but if you need any further explanation, or would like to increase the level of cover you have, please do not hesitate to contact me.

Bullet points in a paragraph

Bullet points can break up a paragraph to help the reader understand and warn the reader of the structure to come. Below, they show there aren't six items in a list of a line or less each, there are actually three items.

Spacing for bullet points:

- This should be consistent, with the same space after the introduction line as between each bullet point.
- There should be less space between the bullet points and the paragraph breaks before and after them.
- The bullet point list should be a clear 'item' together with the introductory line.

In this example, there is a paragraph break after the introductory line and the bullets are then a paragraph on their own. This contradicts the meaning given by the words. There should be the same space after the introductory line as there is between each bullet.

Make sure that the bullet points line up with the introductory line, not having a small indent as above.

Punctuation of bullet points often causes confusion; see the guidance on page 19.

Keep the bullet point list together

Bullet points can break up a paragraph to help the reader understand and warn the reader of the structure to come. Below, they show there aren't six items in a list of a line or less each, there are actually three items.

Spacing for bullet points:

- This should be consistent, with the same space after the introduction line as between each bullet point.
- There should be less space between the bullet points and the paragraph breaks before and after them.
- The bullet point list should be a clear 'item' together with the introductory line.

If the bullet points are short and simple, single-line spacing is fine. If they get longer, they benefit from some space, but this should always be less than a full paragraph break. That means that related information is visually joined.

Make sure that the bullet points line up with the introductory line. as above.

Punctuation of bullet points often causes confusion; see the guidance on page 19 .

Headings

Even if you follow all the principles of general readability with short paragraphs, left alignment, and so on, the document can still look boring and it may not be clear which information is related.

Numbering is used to join related paragraphs together, as well as help with quick reference in meetings. It is generally preferable to use simple numbering: 2, 2.2, (a).

Headings should be descriptive of the content that follows, written in plain English and consistent in style. They support understanding, as the reader knows from the start what the paragraph is about, instead of having to read into it to find out.

Readers will use the headings to find information and, on templates, to help compare across several documents.

Perhaps less obviously, headings guide the reader away from information which is of no interest. If someone starts reading a paragraph and subconsciously decides it isn't relevant, they will jump to the next paragraph and perhaps do so a few times before getting bored. Having headings guides them to where they should start reading again and, hopefully, maintain their interest.

Headings help

Even if you follow all the principles of general readability with short paragraphs, left alignment, and so on, the document can still look boring and it may not be clear which information is related.

1. **Numbering**

   Numbering is used to join related paragraphs together, as well as help with quick reference in meetings. It is generally preferable to use simple numbering: 2, 2.2, (a).

2. **Headings**

   Headings should be written in plain English and be consistent in style.

   2.1 **Describe content**

   They support understanding, as the reader knows from the start what the paragraph is about, instead of having to read into it to find out

   2.2 **Locate information**

   Readers will use the headings to find information and, on templates, to help compare across several documents.

   2.3 **Avoid irrelevant information**

   Perhaps less obviously, headings guide the reader away from information which is of no interest. If someone starts reading a paragraph and subconsciously decides it isn't relevant, they will jump to the next paragraph and perhaps do so a few times before getting bored. Having headings guides them to where they should start reading again and, hopefully, maintain their interest.

Headings should not just be bold text…

1. **Main heading**

If all the headings in your report are the same size, it is not always obvious which are main and which are sub (or sub sub) headings. Where indents are used, this gives some clue, but they are not enough on their own.

1.1 **Second-level headings**

The same is true of the spacing between paragraphs. If it is always the same, it isn't as clear which information belongs together and where a new section starts. This is particularly a problem where there are many headings in a document, with three or four levels of importance.

(a) **Third-level headings**

The problem is worse if the text is fully blocked, all left-aligned as in the next example. After a while, the numbers become more of a visual pattern than a sequence, particularly to people who are more word-focused.

...whether indented or left aligned

1. **Main heading**

   If all the headings in your report are the same size, it is not always obvious which are main and which are sub (or sub sub) headings. The indents give some clue, but they are not enough on their own.

1.1 **Second-level heading**

The same is true of the spacing between paragraphs. If it is always the same, it isn't clear which information belongs together and where a new section starts. This is particularly a problem where there are many headings in a document, with three or four levels of importance.

(a) **Third-level headings**

The problem is worse if the text is fully blocked, all left-aligned as in the next example. After a while, the numbers become more of a visual pattern than a sequence, particularly to people who are more word-focused.

Heading size should reflect importance

1. Main heading

If the visual aspects of typing are to support the message that is being presented by the words, the relative importance of headings and the way the text is broken up into sections should be clear. The headings for the main sections of the report should be one or two points larger than the text used in the paragraphs.

1.1 Second-level headings

The font size for sub-headings should be half or one point larger than the size used for the text. If it is one point larger, the main heading should be one point larger again. If this makes the headings too large for your taste, go up just half a point for each level (as on this page).

(a) Third-level headings

For this example, the headings are half a point larger each time. In the example opposite, they increase by one point a time.

1. Main heading

If the visual aspects of typing are to support the message that is being presented by the words, the relative importance of headings and the way the text is broken up into sections should be clear. The headings for the main sections of the report should be one or two points larger than the text used in the paragraphs.

1.1 Second-level headings

The font size for sub-headings should be half or one point larger than the size used for the text. If it is one point larger, the main heading should be one point larger again (as on this page). If this makes the headings too large for your taste, go up just half a point for each level.

(a) Third-level headings

For this example, the headings are half a point larger each time. In the example opposite, they increase by one point a time.

Don’t accept the default tab stops

1. Default tab stops

Your page will be divided into equally-spaced tab stops by default and often the spacing is less than logical, for example at 1.27cm between tabs. This can be over-ridden to give 1cm or whatever you want, but the spacing is still equal. As the numbers in minutes and reports are not equal, this means that some numbers are far away from their headings, others are crammed too close.

1.1 Equal spacing

Rather than the tab stops being equal, it should be the space between the number and the text that is equal. Move the tab stop for the first section, so the text is the distance from the number that you prefer, then match that space to the following headings.

1.1.1 Don’t make the numbers bold

The numbers are surrounded by white space. If they are bold, the reader’s eye will be drawn to them, rather than to the heading they support.

Note the last point about non-bold numbers

Create tabs so space is more equal

1. Default tab stops

Your page will be divided into equally-spaced tab stops by default and often the spacing is less than logical, for example at 1.27cm between tabs. This can be over-ridden to give 1cm or whatever you want, but the spacing is still equal. As the numbers in minutes and reports are not equal, this means that some numbers are far away from their headings, others are crammed too close.

1.1 Equal spacing

Rather than the tab stops being equal, it should be the space between the number and the text that is equal. Move the tab stop for the first section, so the text is the distance from the number that you prefer, then match that space to the following headings.

1.1.1 Don't make the numbers bold

The numbers are surrounded by white space. If they are bold, the reader's eye will be drawn to them, rather than to the heading they support.

Don't overdo the numbering

2 Assessing user satisfaction

2.1 At present it takes a considerable amount of time to collect the data to respond to a complaint. Quite often the cause of the complaint is apparently minor. Information gained from a survey will show our service from their perspective (rather than ours).

2.2 The survey should be conducted over a period of eight weeks. There are approximately fifty users per day and five of these should be surveyed. Although the choice of users should be random, it is important to achieve a balance of gender, ethnicity and age.

2.3 Methods of assessing satisfaction

2.3.1 Face-to-face interview

The users could be interviewed whilst waiting for their appointment. The interview would take around ten minutes and be conducted by a member of staff from the department. The responses would be noted by the interviewer and summarised back to the user.

2.3.2 Telephone interview

This would basically take the form of the face-to-face interview but be conducted over the telephone. There are two possible approaches:

- to call users within a couple of days of their visit and with no prior warning;
- to select the visitors at the time of their appointment and arrange a convenient time.

Use white space if numbering paragraphs

2 Assessing user satisfaction

2.1 At present it takes a considerable amount of time to collect the data to respond to a complaint. Quite often the cause of the complaint is apparently minor. Information gained from a survey will show our service from their perspective (rather than ours).

2.2 The survey should be conducted over a period of eight weeks. There are approximately fifty users per day and five of these should be surveyed. Although the choice of users should be random, it is important to achieve a balance of gender, ethnicity and age.

Methods of assessing satisfaction

2.3 **Face-to-face interview**

The users could be interviewed whilst waiting for their appointment. The interview would take around ten minutes and be conducted by a member of staff from the department. The responses would be noted by the interviewer and summarised back to the user.

2.4 **Telephone interview**

This would basically take the form of the face-to-face interview but be conducted over the telephone. There are two possible approaches:

- to call users within a couple of days of their visit and with no prior warning;
- to select the visitors at the time of their appointment and arrange a convenient time.

Think about how text is joined/separated

6	**Dress code for office staff** The committee considered adopting a dress code for office staff, particularly as the public will be attending meetings in the building. There were concerns about the difficulty of defining what was acceptable and gaining staff commitment to the idea, so it was decided to ask staff for their opinions before continuing. Email to be sent to all office staff asking for their views on a dress code in principle, and for suggestions as to what should be deemed inappropriate for office wear. To be discussed at November meeting.	**TM [date]**
7	**Training for Office upgrade**	
7.1	**Matters arising** **Training budget** There is no dedicated budget available; any training will need to be provided in-house or come from the general training budget when the training needs have been assessed. **Previous Office training** At the time of the last upgrade, the training was out-sourced to Wardley College but basic outlines were kept by the IT department (attached). Course outlines to be circulated to group members.	**AK [date]**
7.2	**Training for Office 365** The committee were pleased that all staff would have access to Office 365. Staff had varying levels of expertise, so it was decided that a combination of half-day sessions and one-to-one appointments with an IT trainer would be offered.	

Lack of top and bottom cell
Margins 'squash' the text.

Use lines and white space together

6	**Dress for office staff** The committee considered adopting a dress code for office staff, particularly as the public will be attending meetings in the building. There were concerns about the difficulty of defining what was acceptable and gaining staff commitment to the idea, so it was decided to ask staff for their opinions before continuing. Email to be sent to all office staff asking for their views on a dress code in principle, and for suggestions as to what should be deemed inappropriate for office wear. To be discussed at November meeting.	**Tom Marr** [date]
7	**Training for Office upgrade**	
7.1	**Matters arising**	
(a)	**Training budget** There is no dedicated budget available; any training will need to be provided in-house or come from the general training budget when the training needs have been assessed.	
(b)	**Previous Office training** At the time of the last upgrade, the training was out-sourced to Wardley College but basic outlines were kept by the IT department. Course outlines to be circulated to group members.	**Ann King** [date]

Note the better use of bold text and the grey lines for the table.

Summary

In a longer document:

- headings should be bold and sized to reflect relative importance;
- headings of the same level (eg '1', '1.1') should be the same size;
- numbers should not be bold text;
- the space between the number and heading should be the same throughout;
- white space helps to group related information, if there is one blank line between paragraphs, there should be one-and-a-half or two blank lines between sentences;
- If you have to use a table layout, ensure lines are grey, vertical margins inserted and white space is still correctly used.

Tables

Tables are often a better way of giving information than words … but not as often as users think they are. People who don't 'do' numbers will look at them without drawing any information from them. Sometimes the reader is looking at one aspect of the information when the writer intended them to be looking at another.

The default options for presenting tables go against the principles of readability in almost every way with the width stretched to the margins, heavy lines fighting the numbers for attention, zero margins top and bottom leaving figures pressed up and down to the lines.

Another problem can be caused by writers using a 'RAG' system – marking items as red, amber or green to indicate progress against targets. Often the strength of the colours hides the information and contributes to the chaotic look of the table. It is better to have one 'mark' column which is shaded or type text in the coloured font.

Finally, numbers are capital-letter sized and thus can SHOUT at the reader. If you use 12pt text for words, use 10pt text for numbers in the table.

Don’t accept default equal column widths

Location	**Quarter 1**	**Quarter 2**	**Quarter 3**	**Quarter 4**
Abbot Street Practice	132	141	138	198
Leicester HC Street HC	243	249	261	327
Farmers’ Yard Practice	186	188	192	269
Lindon Group Wellbeing	334	332	343	425
Total	**895**	**910**	**934**	**1,219**

Figure 2.4 Missed appointments by practice

Edit the width to suit the content

Location	Quarter 1	Quarter 2	Quarter 3	Quarter 4
Abbot Street Practice	132	141	138	198
Leicester Street HC	243	249	261	327
Farmers' Yard Practice	186	188	192	269
Lindon Group Wellbeing	334	332	343	425
Total	**895**	**910**	**934**	**1,219**

Figure 2.4 Missed appointments by practice

Don't accept default black lines

Location	Quarter 1	Quarter 2	Quarter 3	Quarter 4
Abbot Street Practice	132	141	138	198
Leicester Street HC	243	249	261	327
Farmers' Yard Practice	186	188	192	269
Lindon Group Wellbeing	334	332	343	425
Total	**895**	**910**	**934**	**1,219**

Figure 2.4 Missed appointments by practice

Use grey lines to focus on the content

Location	Quarter 1	Quarter 2	Quarter 3	Quarter 4
Abbot Street Practice	132	141	138	198
Leicester Street HC	243	249	261	327
Farmers' Yard Practice	186	188	192	269
Lindon Group Wellbeing	334	332	343	425
Total	**895**	**910**	**934**	**1,219**

Figure 2.4 Missed appointments by practice

Don’t accept default top/bottom margins

Location	Quarter 1	Quarter 2	Quarter 3	Quarter 4
Abbot Street Practice	132	141	138	198
Leicester Street HC	243	249	261	327
Farmers’ Yard Practice	186	188	192	269
Lindon Group Wellbeing	334	332	343	425
Total	**895**	**910**	**934**	**1,219**

Figure 2.4 Missed appointments by practice

Add a little space above and below the text

Location	**Quarter 1**	**Quarter 2**	**Quarter 3**	**Quarter 4**
Abbot Street Practice	132	141	138	198
Leicester Street HC	243	249	261	327
Farmers' Yard Practice	186	188	192	269
Lindon Group Wellbeing	334	332	343	425
Total	**895**	**910**	**934**	**1,219**

Figure 2.4 Missed appointments by practice

Don't stretch a table unnecessarily

Location	Quarter 1	Quarter 2	Quarter 3	Quarter 4
Abbot Street Practice	132	141	138	198
Leicester Street HC	243	249	261	327
Farmers' Yard Practice	186	188	192	269
Lindon Group Wellbeing	334	332	343	425
Total	**895**	**910**	**934**	**1,219**

Figure 2.4 Missed appointments by practice

Use an appropriate column width

Location	Quarter 1	Quarter 2	Quarter 3	Quarter 4
Abbot Street Practice	132	141	138	198
Leicester Street HC	243	249	261	327
Farmers' Yard Practice	186	188	192	269
Lindon Group Wellbeing	334	332	343	425
Total	**895**	**910**	**934**	**1,219**

Figure 2.4 Missed appointments by practice

Don't leave the reader to work it out

Location	**Quarter 1**	**Quarter 2**	**Quarter 3**	**Quarter 4**
Abbot Street Practice	132	141	138	198
Leicester Street HC	243	249	261	327
Farmers' Yard Practice	186	188	192	269
Lindon Group Wellbeing	334	332	343	425
Total	**895**	**910**	**934**	**1,219**

Figure 2.4 Missed appointments by practice

Guide the reader to the point of the table

Missed appointments rose sharply in quarter four

Location	**Quarter 1**	**Quarter 2**	**Quarter 3**	**Quarter 4**
Abbot Street Practice	132	141	138	198
Leicester Street HC	243	249	261	327
Farmers' Yard Practice	186	188	192	269
Lindon Group Wellbeing	334	332	343	425
Total	**895**	**910**	**934**	**1,219**

Figure 2.4 Missed appointments by practice

All the same principles apply to a text table

13	**Fenshire County Council Update Report** **(Paper CGB2015/094)**	
13.1	**LB presented a verbal report, highlighting three items:** The demographic trend over the next five years showed a 25% increase in the number of people who would need help from adult services. The county council was currently looking at the whole workforce profile, linking with trusts on therapy support and trying to sort pathways. An action plan regarding delayed transfers of care would not be completed before July. The council had a digital strategy trying to make the organisation more effective. It attracted significant investment and this may be of interest to the CCG. The Beechcroft beds were now available and would be short-stay-down beds. The number discharge beds to be confirmed	**LB**
13.	AGREED: The CGB agreed to note the update report	

Grey lines and increased top/bottom margins

13	**Fenshire County Council Update Report (Paper CGB2015/094)**	
13.1	**LB presented a verbal report, highlighting three items:** The demographic trend over the next five years showed a 25% increase in the number of people who would need help from adult services. The county council was currently looking at the whole workforce profile, linking with trusts on therapy support and trying to sort pathways. An action plan regarding delayed transfers of care would not be completed before July. The council had a digital strategy trying to make the organisation more effective. It attracted significant investment and this may be of interest to the CCG. The Beechcroft beds were now available and would be short-stay-down beds. The number discharge beds to be confirmed	**LB**
13.	AGREED: The CGB agreed to note the update report	

A couple of alternative layouts

Location	Quarter 1	Quarter 2	Quarter 3	Quarter 4
Abbot Street Practice	132	141	138	198
Leicester Street HC	243	249	261	327
Farmers' Yard Practice	186	188	192	269
Lindon Group Wellbeing	334	332	343	425
Total	**895**	**910**	**934**	**1,219**

Figure 2.4 Missed appointments by practice

Location	Quarter 1	Quarter 2	Quarter 3	Quarter 4
Abbot Street Practice	132	141	138	198
Leicester Street HC	243	249	261	327
Farmers' Yard Practice	186	188	192	269
Lindon Group Wellbeing	334	332	343	425
Total	**895**	**910**	**934**	**1,219**

Figure 2.4 Missed appointments by practice

Charts & graphs

A well-chosen chart or graph can give clear information that would take a paragraph to explain in words.

Although there are many visual alternatives, it is best to keep to the simple line, pie or bar charts as these are almost always understood. Each has a clear purpose so, as the author, be clear what you are trying to communicate and use the most appropriate means.

A line chart indicates trend, a bar chart shows comparison and a pie chart shows how the whole is made up.

Be careful with your use of colour. Try to have a theme and be aware of colour blindness, avoiding red and green in particular. If the same subjects appear in several graphs, for example, comparing performance of four hospitals, each hospital should have a 'colour' that is the same each time.

A line graph shows trend

Text

The number of missed appointments rose slowly over the first three quarters of the year and increased significantly in the final quarter following the installation of the new phone system.

Graph

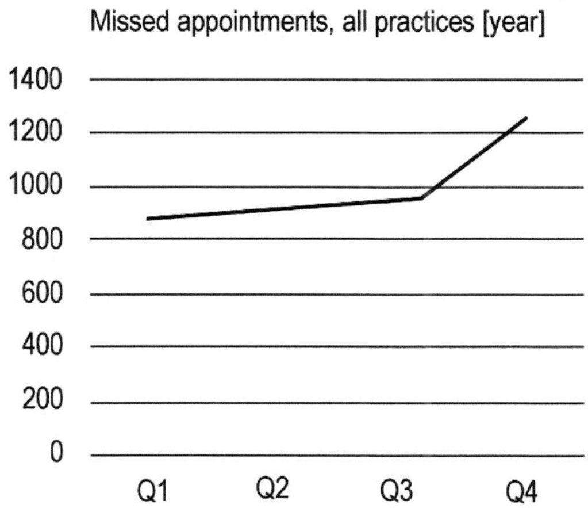

Markers can be put on the chart if you want to draw attention to the points at each quarter; leave them out to place the emphasis on the whole year. Up to three lines can be put on a chart before it risks confusing the reader.

A bar graph shows comparison

Text

Missed appointments in the last quarter were significant higher after the installation of the new phone system compared with the first nine months.

Graph

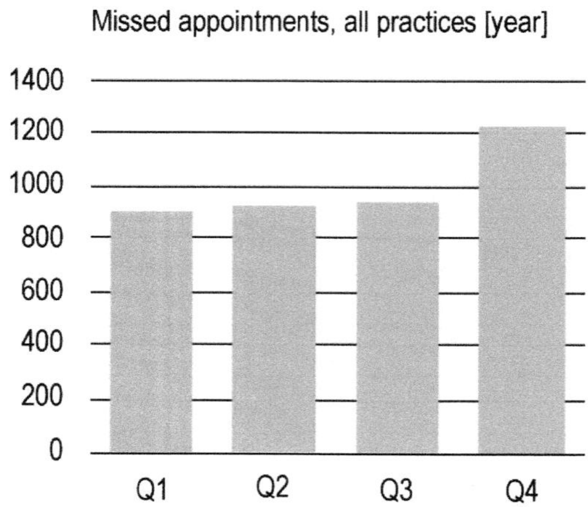

Make sure the bars are wider than the spaces between them.

A horizontal bar chart helps read text

If the text in the report has already introduced the subject to the reader, this point is not so important, but if the chart is where the reasons are first given, a horizontal chart may be clearer.

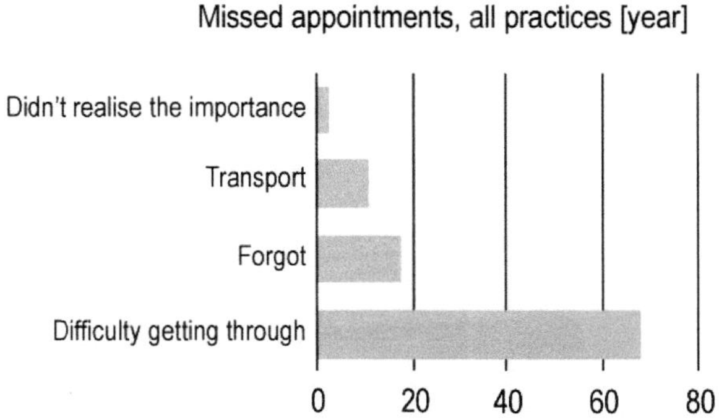

Pie charts show how the whole is made up

Text

Of the reasons given when missed appointments were followed up between February and April, difficulty in getting through was the most common.

Graph

Put the headings around the pie, so the reader doesn't have to keep referring to a separate key.

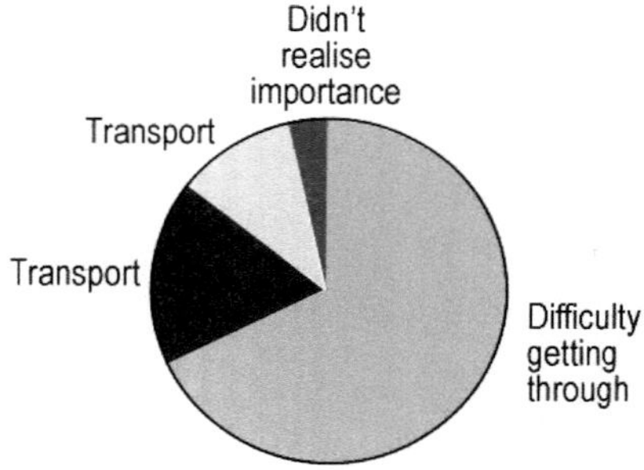

Reasons for missed appointment, Q4

Change the layout if you want to compare

Text

Lindon Group have not yet had the new telephone system installed and there is a noticeable difference in the number of missed appointments caused by difficulty in getting through.

Graph

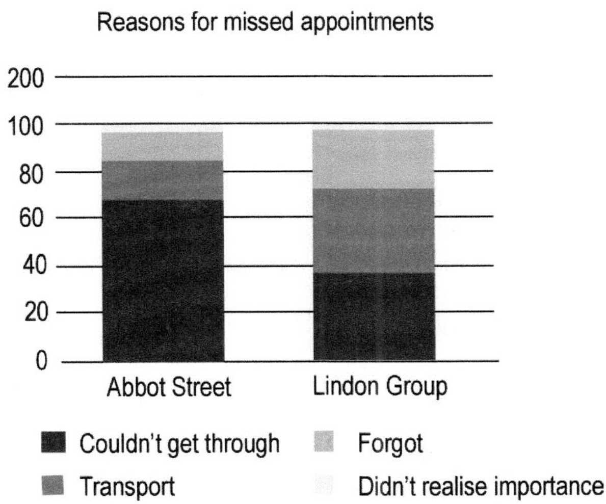

It is difficult to compare information in two pie charts, so change the 'pie' to a 'flapjack' (stacked bar chart) if you want to do this.

Got it? Answers

Stop

❶ Do you want the pack sent to all applicants?

❷ The first applicant for the admin assistant post wanted to know if she would be entitled to a company car! (Or full stop)

❸ Jack wants to know if you want the pack sent to all applicants.

❹ So that I can write up the report, can you tell me on what date was the initial complaint received? How many items did Mr Russell order? How many were faulty? What action did we take after that first letter?

❺ Sarah hit the man.
Sarah hit the man!
Sarah hit the man?
Sarah, hit the man.
Sarah, hit the man!

❻ Would you prefer red or blue?

❼ Do you like the red? Or would you prefer blue?

❽ Alison asked, “Can I claim expenses if I travel to the London office?”

❾ Alice asked if she could claim expenses if she travelled to the London office.

❿ Can I claim expenses if I travel to the London office?

Pause

❶ Please bring the manual, ruler, pens and pencils, calculator and a dictionary.

❷ Please bring the program disc; a copy of the manual on which to make notes; a 30cm ruler; pens and pencils for taking notes and highlighting; a scientific calculator and a dictionary.

❸ In response to your comments, I have arranged to meet all team leaders this week.

❹ All team leaders have responded to the questionnaire with positive suggestions for preventing a recurrence of the fraud.

❺ There are four teams remaining: Barnsley, Bath, Halifax and Reading.

❻ Staff are to get a small bonus this year; directors have elected to receive nothing.

❼ Have you ever received treatment for, or related to, back pain?

❽ There are four teams remaining:
- Barnsley
- Bath
- Halifax
- Reading

❾ The Chief Executive thanked staff for, "...the terrific efforts made to achieve the target."

❿ The four remaining teams are Barnsley, Bath, Halifax and Reading.

Quoting and separating

❶ I enclose a copy of 'My Employment, Terms and Conditions' and would ask you to read through this before you start work with us.

❷ The inspector's report draws attention to, "...large quantities of waste paper stored underneath desks."

or The inspector's report draws attention to, "Large quantities of waste paper stored underneath desks..."

❸ Members of the new leadership team (Chief Executive, Chief Operating Officer and Finance Director) will attend and take questions from staff.

❹ The tutor confirmed, "All students in the cohort [2019] understood what was wanted, and all were happy to comply with the course requirements."

❺ The recording shows that Mr Azim said, "I called customer services on the 23 March at 0942 and was told that a refund would be paid." In response, our team member checked the file and confirmed, "I am able to refund the cost of the printer but not the delivery charge."

❻ Mark Anderson denied the accusation saying, "I have only taken short tea and coffee breaks, and a half-hour lunch break."

❼ "There will be no strike action before Christmas," according to the union representative, "unless there is further provocation from management."

❽ All staff will be invited to attend, although there will be no pressure to do so, and will have the opportunity speak to the inspectors.

❾ Mr Anderson said, “The training [Practical Punctuation], will benefit all staff, it doesn’t matter what they write.”

❿ You can reach us by bus, the airport bus stops outside the door, or by train with a short taxi ride.

Joining

❶ She is a white-car fashionista. You can see her car from here with its go-faster stripes and super-size wheels.

❷ Mother-to-be attacked in front garden.

❸ We can't say it isn't ours – you've signed it on the final page.

❹ They're claiming that their right to live there is being ignored and we haven't been taking their complaint seriously.

❺ Staff will be offered one-to-one appointments with one of our in-house trainers and an in-depth handout will be provided for ongoing reference.

❻ Who's the idiot whose car got stuck under the barrier in the car park? It's not the first time a car has had its roof damaged that way.

❼ Mrs Patel has a walking-stick but her post-operative mobility is generally good.

❽ No-one would co-operate with the enquiry and it was decided that it would be abandonned and the contracts would be re-signed.

❾ Our signed-for service: you can ask for your letter to be signed for at the time of posting to get evidence of delivery.

❿ Her ex-husbands claim is strange as they had agreed to a no-fault divorce and there was a pre-nuptial agreement in place.

Apostrophe and capital letter

❶ According to Mrs Wall's social worker, she and Mr Wall are going to separate.

❷ The tube drivers' strike is likely to cause disruption for three days.

❸ The board discussed the issue of the trust's internet security and were concerned that each hospital had a separate virus protection program.

❹ Over-performance across the CCGs has increased to 3.2%. The highest levels are seen in elective care, critical care and day-case activity.

❺ The NHS's approach to plastic surgery is not consistent and this is reflected in GPs' advice.

❻ The diagnosis of Parkinson's disease led to his medication being changed to Madopar, although this was quickly changed to the generic version, co-beneldopa.

❼ The Government's attitude to private healthcare has been influenced by the Telegraph's campaign after its readers' letters showed their discontent.

❽ Mrs Rafael's symptoms were apparent from last year's assessment according to her GP's notes.

❾ Doctors' training is no more rigorous than dentists', but the public perceive it differently.

❿ Your doctor has recommended that you attend the above cardiac clinic. On your first visit you will be assessed by a specialist cardiac nurse and may also see your specialist.

BV - #0007 - 280319 - C0 - 197/132/5 - PB - 9781907527401